# The Lost Sheep

CW00850890

# Ian Harding

# Contents

# Knowing-All

All is within me
And yet, I have doubt.

All is around me
And yet, I have little faith.

All is what I know
And yet, I fumble at every turn.

All is what I am
And yet, I am forgiven.

All is knowing you
All is loving you
All is my joy and salvation.

## Wonder

As a snowflake taps the nose
As a butterfly kisses a bloom
As an infant's eyes shine
As a thought that fires the heart
As a life of love to live
As a wonder of Nature's way
As a prayer from heaven above.

## A Done Day

It all started
When I was not ready
But there was
A need in the world
And I was chosen.
In life I learnt
That I was not
And never would be
An inclusive….
I am just there
As a warm breeze
That passes through
And cheers the heart.
So life is about
Who you might meet
Along the way
And what a difference
A smile can make
To celebrate
A done day.

## Days of Longing

Across the sea of cries
Over stretching horizons
Of spanked blue
Are the calls for the day after
Whether for the pursuit of love
Or just rewards for good deeds
A plea to the winds of time
Hold dear to those that dream
And shower the humble with kisses
That they may grace their maker's presence
To the world of far and beyond.

## You

When I fall...
You reach.

When I flounder...
You guide.

When I doubt...
You care.

When I yearn...
You love.

When I am lost...
You search.

## Presage

And so it was
And so it will be
And so it is.

So it was
The dawn of Mother Earth
Birthplace of expression
Of colour, of magnificence
Devoid of a single voice.

So it will be
The dawn of a great nation
The seat of power and confusion
A vast landscape of dreams
So many voices, lost to falsehoods.

So it is
Nature's smoky renaissance
Coveted by the heavens
Raging its destructive fury
Only one voice, cries deliverance.

## The Face Of Time

Your face pitted with the worlds crime
Bares all through winds of time
The character shapes and forms
Only to bear the crown of thorns.

Through your glorious ascension
You release the souls of our inner most expression
This now is a new time to begin
Free from temptation, guilt and sin.

True to the good words you say
You did indeed rise on the third day
Mankind is blessed with the gift to try
To learn, live and love as a testament to the one on high.

## In My Way

And in my way
mountains reach

And in my way
oceans roar

And in my way
beasts prowl

And in my way
loves peril

And in my way
heavens grace.

## Defiance

And how the sultry sea
Spits at the jagged
Rock face of defiance
As the wind howls
Its unforgiving laughter
On those un-repenting souls.
The lighthouse warns
By flash and groan
The barricade of faith
One true force
Of Natures swell.

## Living With Faith

Ours, is the duty
Not of choice, or
A sense of responsibility but
Of a feeling nestled deep within.

Ours, is the joy
Not of selfishness, or
A sense of desire to share but
Of a feeling of loving.

Ours, is the living
Not for sake, or
A sense of honour but
Of a feeling of purpose.

Ours, is to praise
Not of concern, or
A sense of desperation but
Of a feeling of humble contriteness.

Ours, is to serve
Not of total release or
A sense of obedience but
Of a feeling to journey.

## Of This World

Of Nature's breeze  -
Flowers are notes
From divine to flesh.
Of the Sun's scattered rays -
Smiles are borne
From one to another.
Of the Gospel rains -
Cover is taken
Nourishing for a better day.
Of the Moon's shine -
Truth is found
As a celebrant to nature.

## Full Circle

Born to this world
Through stained innocence

Living this life
Dressed in blanket beliefs

In passing to
Heavens reclaim.

## Soul-less Moon

I am the soul-less moon
For those that sense the cold light of truth
Yet turn away to darkness.

For those that have feared
Its haunting glare
Yet fail to change paths.

For those that ride
The night's shadows
To never rule the day.

For those that flounder
Will find, I am
The soul-less moon.

## A Most Probable Epitaph

As clouds hush by
The four seasons of my soul
Display like a gallery of paintings
Landscaping glimpses of memory
Through the gaze of recording eyes...

I see the richness of hard work
And the futility of lost opportunity -

I see the wisdom of age
And the wastefulness of youth -

I see the beauty of good deeds
And the portrayals of self-indulgence –

I see the canvas of a fourth season
And the chance to refashion.

## Beyond

I envy not in my mind
But at the far reaches of my soul
For the hearts that serve
Without the need for simple reward
Not knowing that purity
Engulfs their very essence,
Sends me to heights of adoration.

## Overcome

No more the smile
That life bestows

No more the spoken word
That expresses all

No more the furrowed brow
That registers concern

No more the sadness
That mourns a passing

But more the smile
In memory and celebration.

## The Quiet Stand

A ring of mourners stand silent as stone
Heads bowed in quiet deliberate reverence
Some hang out tears, others stare in disbelief
Many simply not there, feelings so immense.

Death adorns black attire cloaking misery
As the husk lays discarded, not forgotten
Out there memories flicker around
Emotions seeping melancholy sound.

Our dear friend outed from precious days
Some hope elevated to peaceful rest
Others confused gripped in collective haze
But spirit of memory relives life's best.

## As We Search

Our souls encased in human frame
Encounter fun and frolics, sadness and pain
Blissfully unaware of mortal danger around
As our fragile existence is hidden bound
It is true that in a blink
Our frames vanish from sight
But so many times, sadly
The good ones go, is that right?
The injustice of it all weighs heavy
As we search for explanation at the ready
Whilst we love, learn and toil with strife
To understand the mystery that's life.

# Faith

Our faith steeped in wisdom and wonder
Transcends all others we are led to believe
Not that we should dare to question our elders
So pause and ask, why do all religions hail supremacy?

Are all our 'one true gods' so very different?
Were we not all placed on earth to find truth?
Our God may have given each, the same set of rules,
differently
So to find the righteous path free from sin.

Could human spirit actually puzzle out the meaning of life?
Over centuries we have learnt very little it seems
The abuse of religion to wretch our guilt on others is
commonplace
So will the human experiment triumph before the end of
time?
Our Maker looks on with tears of hope.

## It Starts Right Here

Perfection is a mind set to journey
Faith is taking one step
And then another.

## Hear See

The night air coated with droplets of dew
Heralds change that no man can ignore.
It is that very normality of nature
That schools our thoughts, our ways
That everything on this good earth
Has its place and time to show.

Like everything in life, it is a guide.
It is up to us as to how we
Respond, react or simply interpret
How we are to make a difference
Recognising that simple beauty, only
If ears receive with wide open eyes.

## So Good

Time presents a memory
Of fallen combatants
Like tens of thousands of
Leaves, torn from living sap
For every conflict, every season
Innocents are blown away
Their supreme sacrifice
So good, now that they have gone.

## Hold Out Your Hand!

Beside the way
Beneath a tree
Sits a lost man, slumped
Staring, staring out at nothing

What could have happened
Upon this very soul
Simply allowing life to drain
To wither from our world

What on earth transpired
For beauty to slip away
Leaving a man to sit in shade
And not this day make hay

May he summon inner strength
And hold out a hand
For one more reaching hope
To bear witness to all that is grand.

## Truth Sings

Even if the sky is falling
And the world goes mad
The mirror of my soul sings...

Even if the winds howl
And the oceans roar with rage
The mirror of my soul sings...

Even if injustice appears to reign
And the wrong people fall
The mirror of my soul sings, truth.

## The Wind Blows

The wind blows
And you are there
As a splice of memory.

The sun glares
And you are there
As a thirsting desert.

The moon beams
And you are there
As the cold look of a statue.

The north star shines
And you are there
As a beacon of truth.

The clouds break
And you are there
Like a sprinkling of sanity.

## Show Me

Show me where shadows lurk
And I will show you a person cowering.

Show me utter self absorption
And I will show you an insular person.

Show me eyes that cannot face you
And I will show you a person that will betray.

Show me a love of money
And I will show you a person rooted in evil.

But show me a true love for the world
And I will show you a soul with a future.

## My Guiding Spirit

I am within
A shell that is
Outwardly known
Expressive yet unnoticed
Three dimensional but flat
This quiet simple being
Does not really understand its purpose
So knocks and knocks and knocks some more
Seeking an angel that would care to listen.

I am now outside
The shell that was
Outwardly known
No expression to notice
Three dimensional but gone
This quiet reflective soul
Begins to understand its purpose
So applauds and applauds and applauds some more
With comfort that an angel cared to listen.

## Taking Account

We live this world
Mirrored through heavenly souls
The life force of pure angels
That take account of daily lives.
The sun shines over
These blessed portals
Lighting the painted path
Recording rights and wrongs
To be presented at our passing.

## Be Ready

What heart
What mind
What soul
Can perceive
What I am bound
To reveal
To you my friend
To you a stranger.

What love
What feeling
What warmth
Can perceive
What I am bound
To release
To you my friend
To you a stranger.

What praise
What prayers
What knowledge
Can perceive
What I am bound
To share
With you my friend
No longer a stranger.

## My Sweet Lord

O sweet Lord of grace
My heart is with thee
I reach to you gladly
For your melody of words
That would sing for the world
Let me be your tears
And your love
Let me be your breath
And your hope
Let me share your blessings
Through your poetic words.

## Made Up

Through the daylight hour
Of my open heart
To the night time hour
Of my inner soul
Forges the true spirit
That will lend itself
To the world.

## Fit For Purpose

Life is a test
Of meaning, understanding
With revelations of truth
At every corner.

## A Wreath

I lay before me a wreath of words
Torn from living dreams, wounded
By a mask of loving lies
So many truths dance
In fire on heavens bridge
Burnt by deeds, ravaged by time
There will be no solace
Save that of visions
Fortified with hope
For love lights the way
Along unpredictable paths
Catching fragments, of
Charred and broken soul
As a renaissance begins.

## Forward March

I understand more than I know –
As for every ending, there is a beginning -
Hidden maybe, but it is there...
I know it is!
And so to the valley of my dreams
Where the tomorrow seeds will grow -
A place of peace with Nature's hand
Reminding an earth laden soul
Of spiritual dawns to break
Revealing glimpse and prospect
The essence of human desire...

## A First Communion

Holy Sacraments once held and versed
Nurturing my kindred spirit
In trust whilst I played
Are now prepared and presented
For my future good works.

It is my time
To learn, to respond
To respect, to reflect
To bear witness.

You have called my presence
You have lit a candle for my soul
A beacon of light shining for you.

I wish now to receive the Sacrament
As one heart
One soul
In one Communion.

# Communion Of Celebration

The whole day the sun shone
Faces alight spreading out their smiles
Beautiful princesses and handsome princes
Excited in staged starched movement
All dressed in the finest regalia
Bearing witness for all to see
On the day the sun shone.

Elders look on in prides place
As the path once trailed, is
Signposted with love and direction
For children's play is to follow
Walking in parallel dimension
In the footprints of the blessed one
On the day the sun shone.

Fresh faces offer hands shaped as crosses
In preparation, reverence and ritual
To receive the body of Christ
And the cupping of the silver chalice
To receive the blood of Christ
Forming a communion with God, his church and people
On the day the sun shone.

## Revelation

If my eyes
Are a window
To my soul
Then my heart
Must be the truest
Reflection of heaven
And my mind
The seed of futures hope
So arise my beleaguered soul
To walk where better feet have run.

# God Knows!

It is human nature
To find fault with others
So why not God?

When human things go awry
It is easy to point fingers
Even towards God?

It is not a perfect world
It was never meant to be
So let's blame God?

Why is it so hard to believe
And so compelling to doubt
God knows!

## Change

You can hear the spoken word
Yet you cannot accept the meaning
You stand quite alone
Viewing the world, differently
Strange this sense of change
Not quite sure where to fit
Life's no longer a playground
Just an orderly queue
Humanity slowly fades
Yet the pureness of light reveals.

## Awareness

My heart never sleeps
The mind ever watchful
For my hidden soul records
A life's declaration of deeds.

## How Can This Be?

It always happens to other people!
It should not have happened to me!
It was not in the script that
I should be standing in queue
At least not yet, but
Here I stand, waiting.

I have climbed the steps of life
And reached the heavenly plain
I say my goodbyes as
I look over my shoulder
At what I have left undone
And there I muse, waiting.

The time marker orchestrates
A relentless uniform pace
Of all that is past, present and future
Though I grapple with remnants of life
My soul is drawn northwards
Where I will witness revelation.

## On This Day

Dance...this day in heaven
As you have never danced before;

Sing out...rising soul
For all to hear your song;

Love...life's riches past
For the beauty it deserves;

Embrace...the new world
For brave souls to reunite.

## Farewell

A misty Sun shone
On the day of farewell
Playful smiles turned sullen
As the casket of memories
Came into view -
And so, your ashes were poured
The waves washed you away
Our tears rolled to the shore.

## Passing

A drifting ghost
Of nature's past
Of rampant spirit
Of beautiful love
Of lost dreams
Of spent life.

## Trapped

In the depths
Forge hands of empathy

In the bowels
Flow guttural foundations

In the dark
Flashes the brilliance of light.

## Pathway

There comes before time
A question that is meaningless
For when the world rushes
What picture do you print –
As the cry of your soul
Knows no stills.
Indeed life blurs away
Screams of lost telemetry –
So pray for the right
To understand your reason
There is a voice in your heart
That will lead you to the truth.

## Who Cares?

Who cares    when all on show is self
Who cares    when lost souls are driven to darkness
Who cares    when human tragedy presents
Who cares    when neighbour denigrates neighbour
Who cares    when global warming threatens
Who cares    when species fail survival
Who cares    when human life is abused
Who cares    when all is said and done
Who cares?

## It Is I

It is I  there when you turn
It is I  that strengthens your faith
It is I  that shines through you.

It is I  that calls out to you in your dreams.

It is I  that shadows your path
It is I  that watches over you
It is I  that shows you the way.

It is I  that loves you like no other
It is I  that embellishes you
It is I.

## I Am

I am out there
So I am, where
It is necessary to be.
I am neither
A beginning or an ending.
I am present
I am future.
No time that passes
Will change a thing.
No wayward thoughts
Will deviate truth.
No spoken words
Will identify out there.
And so, I am.

## The Lost Sheep

What is there behind those grand
Arched doors and coloured windows crossed?
Impenetrable walls of faith perhaps
That move and warm the famished heart.
Dare I be bold and seek to be nourished
And douse my earthly body to cleanse
When I know so many seek amends.
But search I must until the light shows
So that I may follow where he sows.
I hope that I will know his name
Just enough to raise the claim
That I was once a sheep lost
Until the day I bore witness
And carried the cross.

Printed in Great Britain
by Amazon